GRAPE CULTURE

IN

STEUBEN COUNTY.

PREMIUM ESSAY.

ALBANY:
VAN BENTHUYSEN'S STEAM PRINTING HOUSE.
1865.

GRAPE CULTURE.

REPORT COMMITTEE.

The undersigned committee on essays, &c., at the winter meeting of the N. Y. State Agricultural Society, Feb. 8, 1865, report that, the only essay handed in for their examination, is one upon Grape Culture in Steuben county, by the Hon. Goldsmith Denniston. This subject was not one of those for which premiums were offered, and it must therefore be considered that the society is under greater obligations for a work unasked for, but in the opinion of the committee of exceeding value. Mr. Denniston's essay is a very complete work, it has a practical, a suggestive, and an historical value. Admirably arranged, exhausting the subject, minute in instructive detail, it is both a guide to the grape culturist of America, and a record of the rise and progress of a new and important branch of agricultural industry in our country. We recommend that the executive committee award to Mr. Denniston a premium of thirty dollars, being the highest premium offered for an essay by the society; and that they also thank Mr. Denniston for the vast amount of labor and research he has so successfully brought to bear upon this interesting subject.

T. L. HARISON,
J. STANTON GOULD,
H. TEN EYCK FOSTER,
Committee.

February 9, 1865.

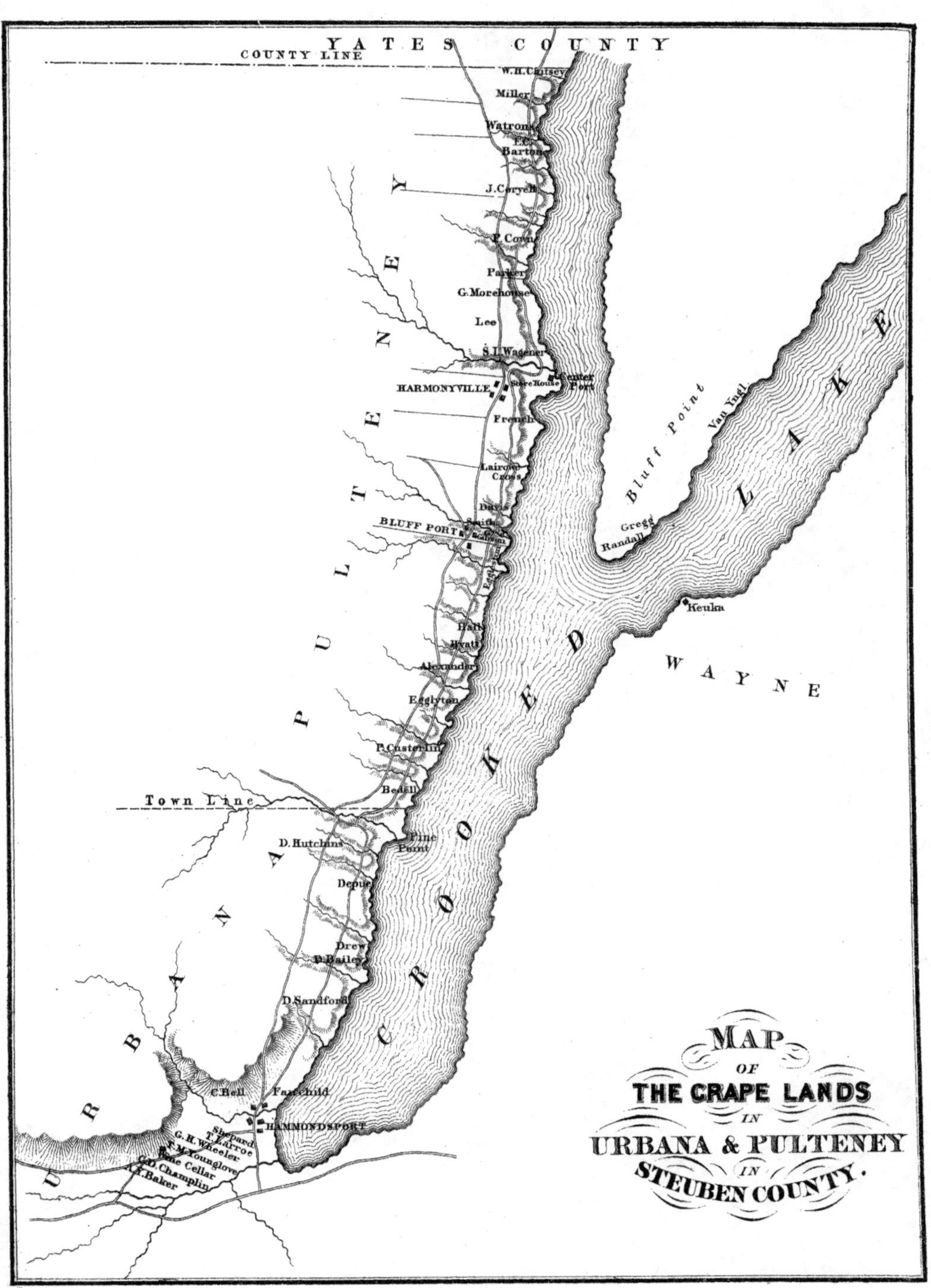

MAP OF THE GRAPE LANDS IN URBANA & PULTENEY IN STEUBEN COUNTY.
YATES COUNTY
COUNTY LINE
Miller
Watrous
Barton
J. Coryell
Parker
G. Morehouse
Lee
S. L. Wagener
Center Port
Store House
HARMONYVILLE
French
Cross
Davis
BLUFF PORT
Hall
Hyatt
Alexander
Egglyton
P. Custerlin
Bedell
Town Line
Pine Point
D. Hutchins
Depue
Drew
D. Bailey
D. Sandford
C. Bell
Fairchild
HAMMONDSPORT
Shepard
T. Larroe
G. H. Wheeler
F. M. Younglove
Stone Cellar
G. D. Champlin
PULTENEY
URBANA
CROOKED LAKE
Bluff Point
Gregg
Randall
Keuka
WAYNE

[From Transactions New York State Agricultural Society, 1864.]

GRAPE CULTURE
IN
STEUBEN COUNTY.

BY G. DENNISTON, PRATTSBURGH.

Previous to the year 1852, the vine received but little attention in this section of the State. Some gardens had one or two vines, which grew untrimmed and uncared for, running over the fence, or perhaps over the limbs of a tree. If they produced fruit it was used for "*preserves,*" and hardly an individual deemed it worthy of keeping "*for the winter*" for "*table use*"—so little *taste* had the good people for this, the richest and most wholesome of all fruits.

It was the current opinion that our climate was unfavorable to the production of grapes that were of any value as an article of food or for the manufacture of wine; that, what was grown would be deficient in sugar, and in the "*aroma*" peculiar to the perfectly matured article. The opinion also appertained that the European grape, of France, Spain, Italy and Germany, were the only varieties that were worthy of cultivation; and as these failed in our climate, the inference drawn was that "we could not grow grapes."

We had extremely imperfect ideas of the capacity of our climate for the growth of the vine, as well, in every respect, for its requirements. We did not understand that "*temperature*" is not a precise guide, but that other conditions also govern; and although our climate exceeds in *humidity* the vine-growing districts of Europe, yet, our atmosphere is drier as a mean, and is certainly more dry and elastic.

This alternation between humidity and dryness is probably the reason that the European grape will not flourish in our climate, and consequently these varieties are very much restricted in our country, particularly, east of the Rocky mountains.

It is known that in Europe the cultivation of the vine has been pushed to the extreme limits of climatic capacity, and in sheltered valleys it is grown successfully far north of other places too cold and variable for its production.

M. Blondeau, writing on the subject of grape culture says, "The determination of the conditions of climate in which the culture of the vine is possible, is of practical as well as theoretical interest. Knowing that any particular locality has long been devoted to this culture we are able to fix the mean temperature thereof, and by studying the circumstances prejudicial to the development of the vine, avoid the failures so often experienced by those who undertake this culture where it is impossible."

"The grape requires four months, or one hundred and twenty days, to come to maturity; we can calculate the aggregate of temperature required to perfect its growth. Bordeaux, in France, being in latitude 44° 50′, has a mean temperature in spring of 56°, in summer of 71°, in autumn of 58°; mean for spring, summer and autumn of 62° 40′. And, as Bordeaux is near the centre of the wine districts of France, a data is furnished, other things being equal, of the climate required for the cultivation of the vine."

It is an interesting study to investigate the particular features of the various vine-growing districts in Europe and the United States, and to notice that neither latitude, nor elevation, nor the amount of rain falling governs, but that other causes combine to render the cultivation certain and profitable. Also, to notice that the range of temperature is not so much controlling as we are inclined to believe. The grapes of Astrachan are said to be equal to the best of Italy, and the range of temperature there is more extreme than in many places of our own country.

Astrachan is in latitude 46° 21′, on a level with the sea; has a mean temperature in spring of 52° 6′, in summer of 75° 9′, in autumn of 52° 4′, in winter 19° 2′; making a mean for the year 50°.

California is undoubtedly the most favorable for grape culture of any part of the United States. The vineyards there produce, ordinarily, twice as much as the vineyards of any other grape district. The crop never fails, as it does in every other country. The soil is a deep, sandy loam, and in some places a rich, black loam and a gravelly clay. The climate is dry and uniform, which insures the grape from rot or mildew.

The mean temperature of California for January is 44.2, for February 45.4, for March 53.4, for April 54.8, for May 62.7, for June 69.1, for July 69.4, for August 71.3, for September 71.1, for October 65.4, for November 54.9, for December 46.2; the spring average being 56.9, the summer 69.9, autumn, 63.8.

A writer on the meteorological conditions necessary to the production of grape wine of the best quality, says, "In addition to a summer and an autumn sufficiently hot, it is indispensable that at a given period—that which follows the appearance of the seeds—there should be a month, the mean temperature of which does not fall below 66.2, Fahrenheit."

September and October in California has a mean temperature of 68.2, maturing the grape with sufficient sugar to make the fruit luscious and the wine rich and of the very best quality; consequently, the wines of that state come nearer to the wines of Italy than any produced upon the American continent.

The soil of the grape-growing district in the county of Steuben is peculiarly adapted to the cultivation of the vine; the geological formation being of the Chemung sandstones and shales, disintegrated to a great depth and full of crevices, through which the water can pass, indicates a soil free from the action of surface water, and consequently warm and loose. Another peculiarity marks the district in this, that deep ravines pass from the hill tops into the valley, making a perfect drainage of the intervening space, and an exposure the most favorable to secure a high temperature in summer and autumn. Many of the headlands present a surface at right angles with the sun's rays, and receive a temperature much higher than their latitude and elevation would otherwise warrant.

This district being on the slope of the west shore of the Crooked lake, a sheet of water of great depth and of unusual purity, which remains unfrozen the most of the winter season, it softens the extreme cold, protects the incipient vegetation of spring, and prolongs the growing season in autumn, by preventing the recurrence of early frosts. The effect of the waters of the lake is that of an equalizing influence upon the temperature, rendering it less liable to sudden changes and more adapted to the growth and maturity of the finer varieties of grapes and fruit.

The mean temperature of the period during which the growth and maturation of the grape takes place, exercises a remarkable influence, and the more uniform the temperature, at the requisite figure, the more certain will the grape mature to the requisite perfection.

It is known that the recurrence of frosts in September and the begining of October, will injure the grape so as to render it unfit for the table, and the wine made scarcely drinkable. It is very essential that the ripening process of the grape be not retarded or interrupted by a low temperature or the occurrence of early frosts.

The peculiar formation of the slope of the west shore of the Crooked lake, secures a temperature even, and extended into October, ripening the grape to the requisite maturity to produce good wine. As an illustration, we present a map of the "Pine point farm," showing the ravines through which the water passes into the lake, and the slope of the hills and intervening ridges. It is deemed a fair specimen of the grape lands of the county.

The hills in this vicinity rise in regular slope, or in a succession of terraces some four hundred feet; back of which are farm lands of great fertility, and hills five and six hundred feet in their rear. The soil of these hills is a shaly loam, mixed with clay; it is open, free, and extremely warm, receiving the sun's rays directly; and in mid-winter the temperature is mild and equable, the lake scarcely freezing over. It is one of those sunny, warm spots where the snow drifts are scarcely seen and the cold blasts are hardly felt. There is a spring atmosphere prevailing here when upon the hills above winter reigns with all its accustomed rigor and severity. In such secluded nooks the grape delights to grow, and by suitable cultivation yields abundant crops of the choicest varieties.

A vineyard has been planted upon this property, and it is the intention of the proprietors to appropriate the whole (168 acres) to the cultivation of the vine.

About the year 1830 the Rev. William Bostwick set some vines at Hammondsport, which grew and produced fine crops. The varieties were the

Isabella and the Catawba. He succeeded in raising these varieties of grapes in perfect maturity, but beyond his efforts none were made in that vicinity for years. About 1843 William Hastings terraced the side hill west of the village of Hammondsport, for a garden, and planted therein vines of the Isabella and Catawba grapes, from which he realized a succession of fine crops. From that time onward to 1855, Mr. Hastings' garden yielded the principal returns of grapes, except it be a few vines scattered through the village. And his fruits and vegetables were the admiration of the citizens of all the surrounding country.

The first attempt to plant a vineyard was made by Andrew Reisinger, a German, who by profession was a vine-dresser, being brought up to the business in Germany. He came to Harmonyville, in the town of Pulteney, in 1853, and selected a bluff, upon which he planted about two acres, and succeeded in producing good crops of Isabellas and Catawbas. He trenched the soil, and cultivated the vine as in his native country, not allowing it to form large branches, but trimmed it down, so as to have the bearing canes near the ground, the fruit receiving the benefit of the reflected rays of the sun and the heat radiated from the soil. He trained his vines to stakes, and did not permit them to grow more than four feet in height; and where they were trellised they were kept of the uniform height of from three to four feet, in the form of a low trellis as here represented.

This vineyard is now owned and occupied by D. S. Wagener, Esq., of Pulteney; and having been enlarged, is in fine bearing condition. The grapes of the present year (1864) have been a full crop, and of a very fine flavor.

The scenery adjacent to this vineyard on the south is more than rural, it is picturesque. A deep ravine cuts the hill asunder to the depth of more than one hundred feet, through which roars the waters passing from the hills. In summer it is the babbling brook; in spring, and time of flood, the fearful torrent, carrying rocks, trees and rubbish down to the flats below. We give a map of the location, from actual survey. It is in character with many other places on the lake shore.

South of Mr. Wagener's is the vineyard planted by C. C. Baldwin, Esq. It contains about one acre, and is in fine bearing condition. Mr. Baldwin has lately sold it, together with about ten acres of land and a small cottage house, for two thousand dollars, which the purchaser deems a good bargain. Mr. Charles Wixam is the present owner.

Mr. Prentice has a fine vineyard south of this, on the slope of the hill, towards the lake shore. He has been a successful cultivator of the grape for many years, and a ramble through his grounds gives one an idea of the pleasure arising from a view of beautiful scenery and of rural taste. These vineyards all repay their proprietors for all the care and the labor they bestow.

The first vineyards started in Pleasant Valley proper was in 1855, by Hon. Jacob Larrowe and Orlando Shepard, each of whom planted about

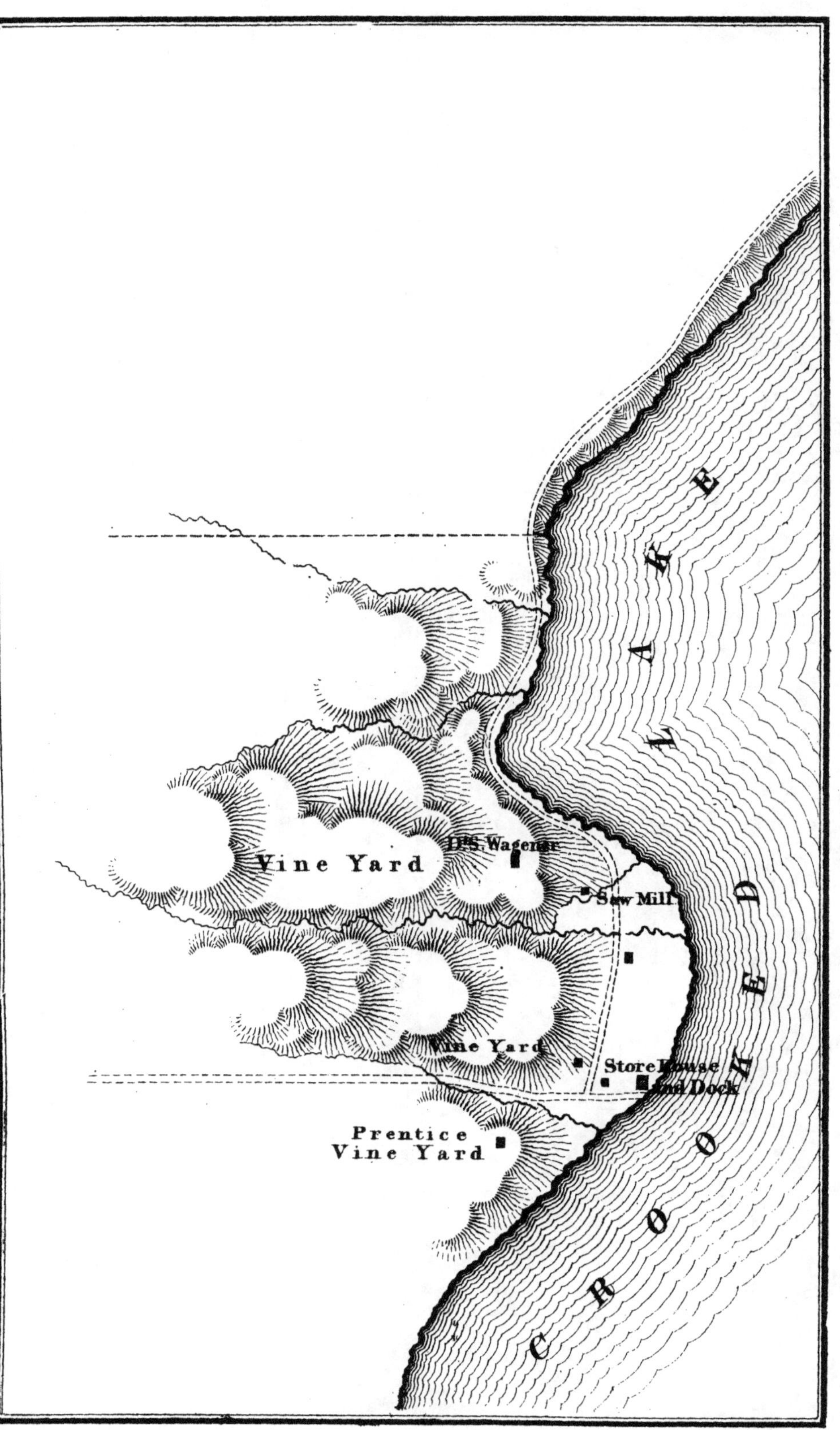
Dr. S. Wagenar
Vine Yard
Saw Mill
Vine Yard
Store House
and Dock
Prentice
Vine Yard
CROOKED LAKE

half an acre, on the slope of hills south-west from Hammondsport. They procured their vines (Isabellas and Catawbas) from Avon, in Livingston county. The soil selected for their vineyards was of a character peculiarly adapted to the growth of the vine, being dry, porous and of extremely easy tillage. It is a gravelly loam with a substrata of shale, the debris of which is largely incorporated in the soil. In this soil the roots of the vine take deep hold, and the canes grow with great luxuriance. They trained their vines to trellis, allowing them to grow to the height of about six feet, in rows about eight feet apart. They kept the ground free from grass and weeds, and usually well tilled. Sometimes they planted beans between the rows, which produced enough to compensate for the dressing. These two vineyards were so productive as to induce others to turn their attention to the business, and thence arose a department of productive industry heretofore unknown in those parts. Finding that their vineyards were successful in the production of crops, both Shepard and Larrowe set out two or three acres more in 1858, and their success induced others to embark in the business and thus extend the area of grape culture throughout the valley.

Clark Ball, Esq., in connection with Judge McMaster, set out about six acres, on the bluff, adjacent to the village of Hammondsport. Grattan H. Wheeler purchased the Decker farm, south of Judge Larrowes', and planted four acres upon the gravelly ridge north-east of his residence. Charles D. Champlin set out one acre upon the rise west of the wine cellar, where the slope is to the south-east. Timothy M. Younglove set out one acre upon a warm bluff, where the sun's rays had full force and the bleak winds were shut out. S. B. Fairchild planted his vineyard upon the lake shore, just north of Hammondsport, in terraced rows, giving a fine, warm exposure, where the fruit matured finely, and the yield was abundant. His vineyard occupied one acre, which has since been much enlarged. Mr. Edwin P. Smith also set out two acres upon the rise adjacent to the village, south of the stone mill, and succeeded in raising fine grapes.

Aaron Y. Baker, having examined the vineyards of Cincinnati and of Kelly's Island, opposite the city of Sandusky, in Ohio, purchased cuttings at the latter place and brought them home with him. A stimulus was thus presented to the citizens of the valley, who entered with renewed zeal into the business of cultivating the grape. Mr. Baker planted his vineyard south-west of the wine cellar, where the hills break towards the west, affording a fine exposure to the south, and securing quite, or more than an average from year to year. His crop, in 1862, yielded over 9,000 pounds to the acre, while the average throughout the valley is placed at 4,000 pounds. The vines procured by Mr. Baker and planted, were chiefly the Catawbas and the Isabellas.

The vine requires for its growth a warm exposure, though not too hot, and a moderate degree of moisture. This condition is found to exist in a high degree upon the slope of the hills adjacent to the Pleasant Valley and to the west shore of the Crooked lake. The banks of the lake shore and of the various gulleys through which the water passes down to the valley and the lake are especially favorable to the grape. These gulleys, made by the torrents of the waters gushing from the plateaus, afford complete protection to the vine; and the formation of the soil is such as to require but little culture beyond the initial preparation of the soil for the reception of the roots.

Most of the vineyards of which we have made mention have been set with cuttings, which being put into the earth, (which has been made rich, and deeply tilled,) from three to four inches apart, and being mulched when the weather is too dry, they strike roots, and are fit the next spring to set in the vineyard.

Some few have propagated the vine by layers: the shoots near the ground are fastened down below the surface of the ground, and the eyes will strike roots, and being cut asunder, form distinct vines, ready to set the next year in the vineyard.

Where extremely scarce varieties are desired, they are obtained by single buds, or eyes. These are caused to grow in a warm apartment, under glass, where the temperature is warm and uniform. The most sure process to start the eyes is by a *bottom heat* of sand, where the eyes are placed and forced to strike roots.

The soil selected for the vineyard, if a side hill, has been generally terraced into distinct plateaus, but some, where the slope would allow, set their vines without this preparation, and by various means have rid the surface of water, and their vineyards grow finely.

Some have planted their vines in rows, not more than six feet apart, while others have made the space ten feet. This latter is deemed much the best for the Isabellas and Catawbas, as they are strong growing varieties, forming an abundance of wood.

The most common mode of training the vines have been on "*trellises*," and principally upon the "*low system.*" The young vine is pruned back to two eyes, as at A, from which two shoots are obtained the following summer, as at B B.

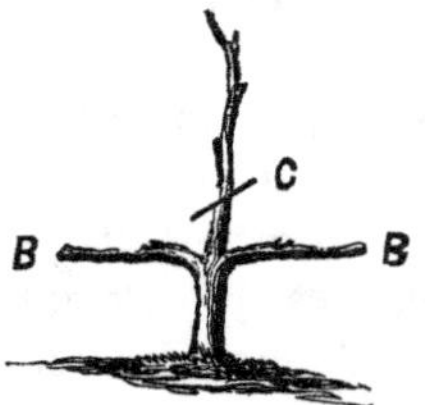

By cutting, the season following, the vertical shoot at C, the vine will form shoots as follows :

These, with proper management, are trained upon the trellis and made to produce fruit and to form wood, as the cultivator may desire. The usual course is to have fruit-bearing arms and wood-growing arms each year, in order to secure full crops from year to year successfully.

The trellis is formed by setting posts into the ground some ten or twelve feet apart and passing three wires of suitable size (say No. 12) between them. This forms a reliable and substantial

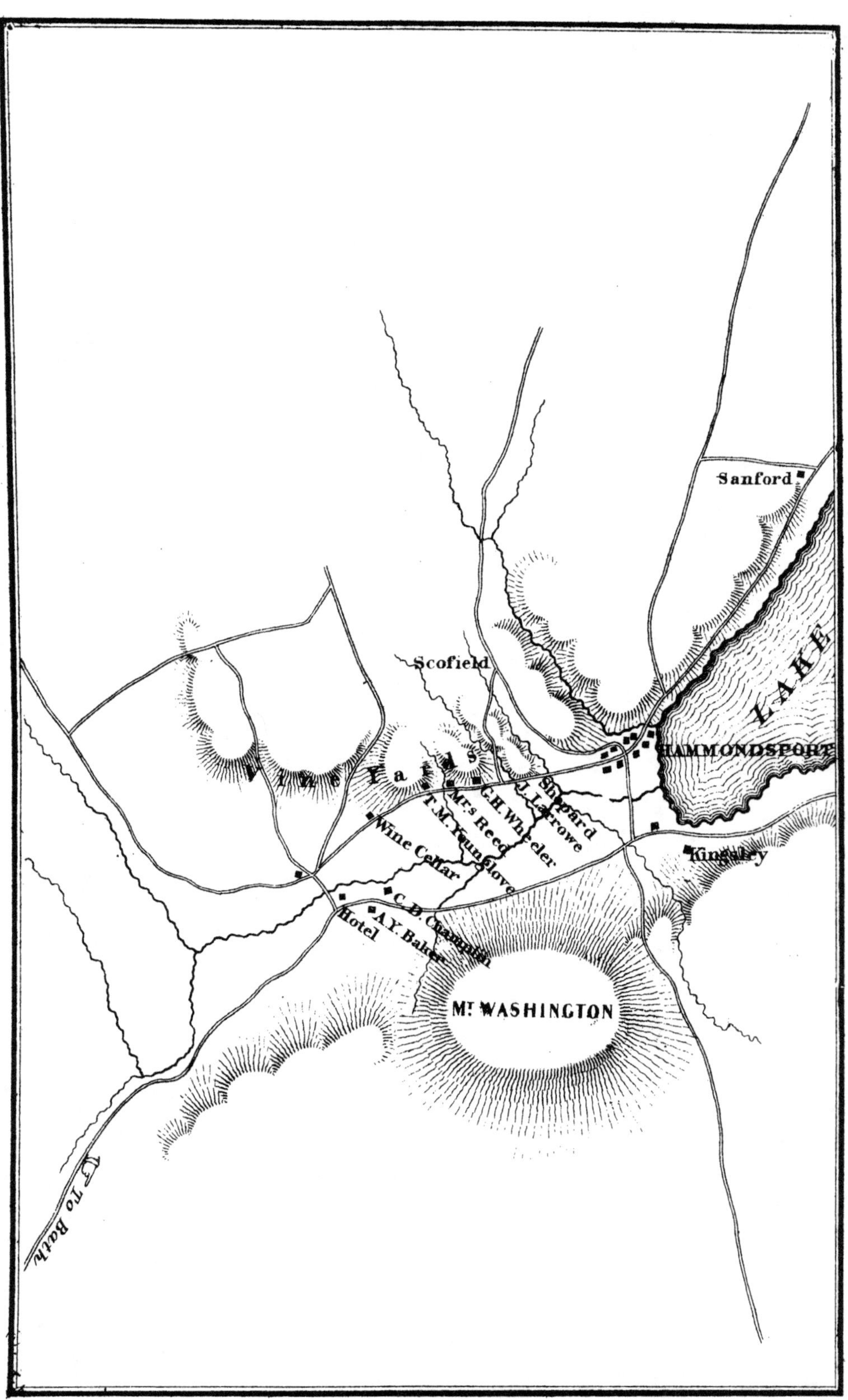

Sanford
LAKE
HAMMONDSPORT
Scofield
Vine Yards
Sheppard
J. Larrowe
G.H. Wheeler
Mrs Reed
T.M. Younglove
Wine Cellar
C.D. Champlin
A.Y. Baker
Hotel
Kingsley
Mt WASHINGTON
To Bath

support to the vine. Some drive stakes into the ground and nail slats, one inch by three, upon them, which forms a temporary support, but they soon decay and have to be renewed.

Some of the most careful cultivators of the grape train their vines upon the *low trellis* in such a manner that the bunches of grapes will be near the ground and receive the warmth radiated from the surface, which insures an early maturity and a rich flavor to the fruit. The grapes growing near the surface of the ground are generally found to ripen sooner, to ripen more thoroughly, and to exhibit more of "*the aroma*" which is produced at a *certain stage* of the maturity of the grape; which, if not arrived at, *no aroma* is discovered, or which, if interrupted at the precise stage, it is greater or less, as the case may be.

The perfect maturity of the grape is of more importance than many cultivators are willing to admit, and the difference in this respect is very discernable in the different vineyards of Pleasant Valley and the lake shore. Some are quite willing to risk the *quality* of their crop for the sake of the *quantity* produced, and allow their vines to grow too much to wood, to be trained too high; while a few discerning and careful cultivators rely more upon the *quality* and train their vines accordingly.

In an examination of the vineyards of Pleasant Valley, in the autumn of 1862, by request of the State Agricultural Society, and with a committee of its appointment, this *difference* of *training* was noticed particularly in the effect it had upon the *aroma* of the fruit. The vineyard of CHARLES D. CHAMPLIN was strictly trained *low*, and many of the bunches hung within a foot of the surface of the ground; these were noticed as being fully ripe and rich in *aroma*, while some, three feet higher, were still unripe and extremely acid. Other vineyards were noticed to present ripe, aromatic fruit, or be deficient therein as the training was low or high.

We present the above observation as of great importance to cultivators of the vine, as the quality of their grapes are valued for the table, as well as for wine, in proportion to the peculiar flavor they possess, derived from the aroma they contain.

Pruning has for its object the formation of the plant and the direction of the flow of the sap. As the vine bears best on branches which come from the wood of the previous year's growth, wood of a similar character must be produced for the next year's crop.

The wire trellis is represented as follows:

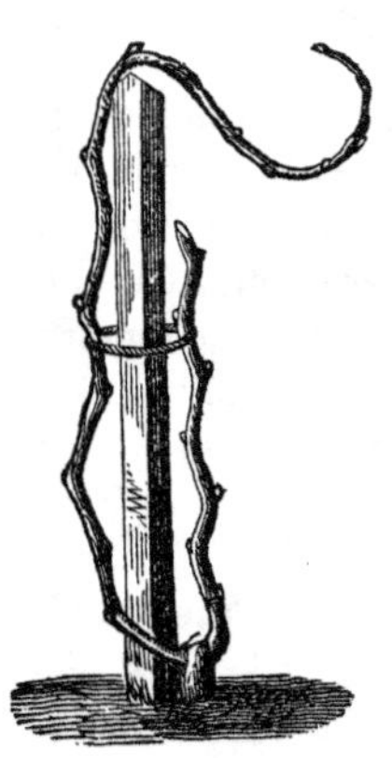

The training of the vine to a single stake allows some diversity, which the careful cultivator will pursue as the crop and his fancy may dictate, but the absolute rule is always to be observed: to trim and to train in such a way as to furnish bearing branches for each year, and to allow the grapes sufficient air and sunshine. The simple stake training, without any pretence to fancy, is as follows:

But the bow and stake system allows of more diversity in form, and, when properly pursued, will furnish more wood from which to produce fruit, and thus secure a larger crop.

The "double bow" is based upon the same principle, but is faulty in its results, as it retains too much wood.

The objects of each mode of training should be the equal diffusion of sap throughout the length of the vine and a steady growth of all the buds, so as to produce a large growth of fruit from the bearing wood, and to remove that to give place to new wood for succeeding crops.

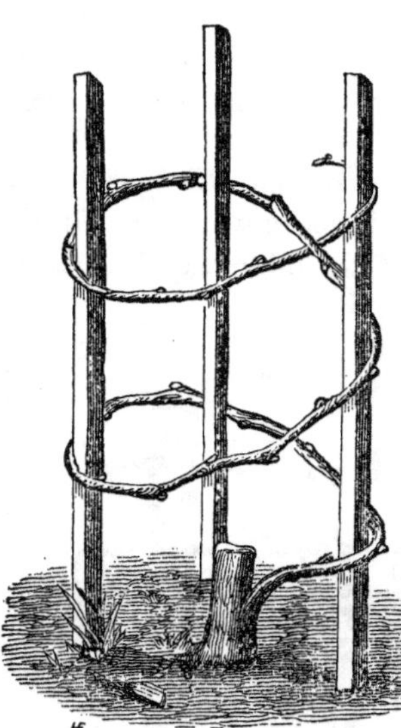

We give also a view of the spiral form of training. It is claimed to admit more air and light within the branches.

The following represents the distaff system of training. It is very pretty, by way of variety, and suits some species of vine that grow "twiggy," but it requires great skill in sustaining the system throughout so as to produce good fruit. In the primeval forests of our country, we found the native vine growing in festoons upon the trees, and to the extent, so as to cluster along the topmost branches. Some of these vines were found to produce extremely good fruit, white, blue and creamy in color, of a rich, sweet flavor, though to *modern* palates would be deemed rather "too foxy."

The Isabella will grow and ripen fine crops upon trees, probably more so than any other variety.

The Italian grapes are trained upon the trees. In the language of the poet, after they have obtained sufficient root and stalk,

> "They brave the winds, and, clinging to their guide,
> On tops of elms at length triumphant ride."

The *aroma* of the grape is no doubt produced by the skin, in connection with the acids formed during the stage of ripening, and such grapes as are possessed of the most perfect aroma produce wines of a peculiar rich flavor, known under the name of "*bouquet*," and all the wines of that grade have a favorable reputation throughout the world.

If the grape does not ripen fully it becomes too acid to be relished, and, in keeping, becomes too watery, and, consequenty, musty, in which condition it is without flavor, and, consequently, the cultivator should notice the peculiar conditions under which his crops are improved or deteriorated.

Some of the vineyards of Pleasant Valley and along the shore of the lake were kept in perfect order, regard was had to the roots as well as to the stems, to keep them in conformity with each other. Where the soil was not naturally loose, it was thoroughly tilled so as to allow the roots to strike deep into the soil. Other vineyards were noticed to be much neglected in this respect, as though their proprietors did not recognize the influence which the roots had upon the grapes, and, consequently, upon the wine, or the benefits derived from "*root pruning*" equal with that of the branches.

The old Romans understood all this in the cultivation of their vineyards, and one of their authors write :

> "Be mindful, when thou hast entomb'd the shoot
> With store of earth around to feed the root,
> With iron teeth of rakes, and prongs, to move
> The crusted earth, and loosen it above."

The training of the vines to stakes is not usual in the vineyards of which we have made reference. Yet many of the German cultivators advocate that system as being the mode of pruning and training in their native land.

Where the vines are trained upon stakes, they need not be set more than six feet apart, as the intervening spaces will permit sufficient sunshine and air to enter to secure early and full maturity to the grape.

The vineyard planted by Mr. REISINGER, in Pulteney, of which we made mention, was trained in this manner, and was not allowed to exceed *five feet* in heighth. But the prevailing mode is the *trellis*.

The cultivation of the vine had become so much extended in Pleasant Valley and along the shore of the lake, that, to ensure a steady market for their grapes, it became important to organize a company for the manufacture of wine and brandy. Heretofore they had depended upon markets at a distance and experienced much inconvenience in the sale of their crops, and very often a great depreciation in the transit of their grapes to the market.

In the year 1860 the association known as the "PLEASANT VALLEY WINE COMPANY" was formed, with a capital of ten thousand dollars. Those who were active in organizing the company were Charles D. Champlin, William Baker, Aaron Y. Baker, T. M. Younglove, G. H. Brundage, Delos Rose, Grattan H. Wheeler, Clark Bell, J. W. Davis, D. McMaster and Dugald Cameron.

The company secured the services of John F. Weber as superintendent to manage the details of the wine and brandy manufacture, as also of the propagation of vines for sale and for future vineyards. Mr. Weber, being a German by birth and education, had acquired great experience in grape culture and in the manufacture of wines and brandies. Aside from this, he was a man of refinement and general intelligence, bringing with him all those qualifications calculated to ensure success in the department of business to which his services were called.

Under the supervision of Mr. Weber the company erected a spacious wine-vault—a press house. They procured a suitable distillery for the manufacture of brandy, also a wine-mill, of the Hickock patent, and erected a house for the propagation of vines. These were all kept in fine working condition by Mr. Weber, and the success of the company was so great as to induce them to double their capital in 1862.

In 1860, when the company was formed, Catawba grapes were sold for six cents per pound and Isabellas at four cents. The present year, 1864, the former brought nine cents and the later six cents. Fine Catawbas are now worth thirty cents in New York.

The first vintage of the company, in 1860, was made from 35,990 pounds of grapes ; the second from 38,988 pounds ; the third from 271,825 pounds ; that of 1863 from 192,467 pounds ; and the fifth vintage, 1864, of about 500,000 pounds. In 1862 the company manufactured 10,967 gallons of wine and 3,403 gallons of brandy ; in 1863 9,844 gallons of wine and 1,418 gallons of brandy ; in 1864 about 30,000 gallons of wine and brandy in the same proportion of excess of previous years. In making the wine and brandy the company have used up about *one-third* of the entire crop grown in the valley ; the balance has been marketed for table use.

They have made wines of the Still, Catawba, Isabella and Claret. They have also commenced the manufacture of champagne from the Catawba grape. In connection with the manufacture of wine, they have manufactured brandies—white brandy (medicinal), Otard brandy, and Cogniac brandy, all of the purest and best grades.

Their wines and brandies are obtaining a wide reputation for purity and flavor. All the wines made in 1860, 1861 and 1862 are sold, and most of the 1863 vintage. Their brandies have been sold about as fast as manufactured, and they find it difficult to fill the accumulating orders.

Aside from the grapes sold to the company, large quantities of the very choicest are put into boxes and sold in the city and village markets for table use. These bring an advanced price, fifteen to thirty cents per pound, according to quality. The vine cultivators feel that they have really found an "ELDORADO" in all the good times and circumstances by which they are surrounded.

An important branch of the vineyard attendance is the gathering of the fruit *at the proper time.* When the fruit is ripe and its juice has attained

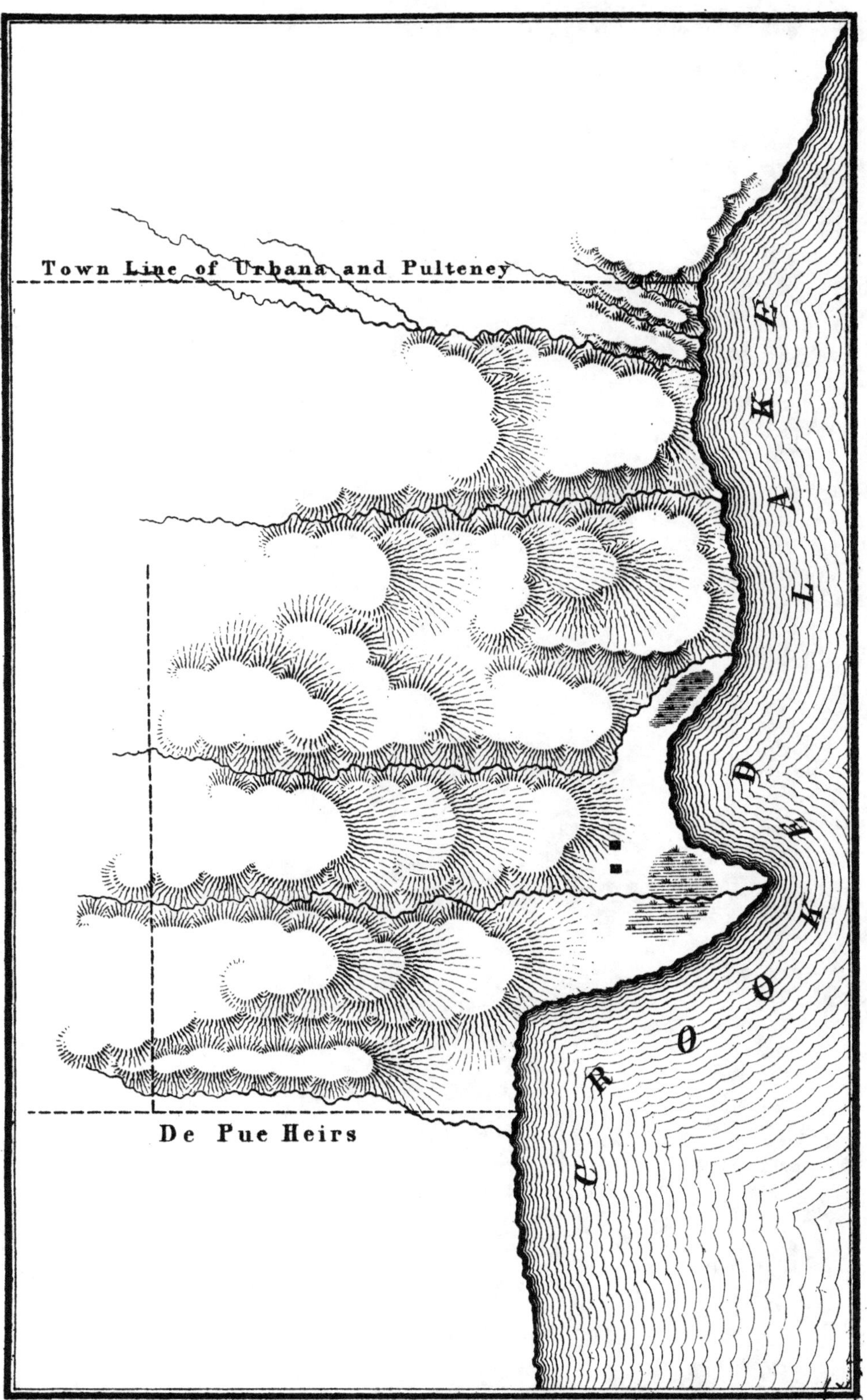
Town Line of Urbana and Pulteney
De Pue Heirs
CROOKED LAKE

its peculiar "*vinous taste*," and the bunches are surcharged with a rich "*aroma*," in this state the grapes are in a good condition to be gathered. This should be done quickly and in dry weather. The usual vessels used in the gathering of the grapes is a wooden pail and a tub of a size easily carried when filled, and larger tubs in which to transport the grapes to the wine cellar. The choice bunches, intended for marketing for table use, are put into boxes of from eight to twelve pounds capacity and nailed tight.

When the grapes are taken to the wine-cellar and weighed, each man receiving credit for all he brings, they are then run through the grape mill into a large vat beneath, called the "*fermenting vat*." By drawing off the juice directly from the vat and putting it into casks to ferment, the product is *white wine*, which is far more pure and agreeable than that obtained from the husks. That which is left in the vat is "*watered*" and allowed to ferment, is distilled into brandy, or, being watered with sugar dissolved therein, by means of which the husks are thoroughly soaked, these being pressed, produces *red wine*—the color being contained in the skin. The wine is put into large casks, of about fifteen hundred gallons capacity, made of sound white oak staves in the most substantial manner. These casks are thoroughly purified before the wine is put in, and, when emptied, is washed clean, then "well sulphured and bunged up."

In the manufacture of "*Claret wine*," the mode in use in France is pursued, as described by Lenoir, and is as follows: "The grapes are mashed in a large vat, containing about twelve hundred gallons, when filled a cover of boards is put over it and the whole, juice and husks, left to ferment. The husks are pressed down twice a day into the juice, and a temperature of sixty degrees is maintained as long as the fermentation continues—about fifteen or twenty days. The wine is then drawn off and put into casks into the cellar, where the fermentation continues until the wine is perfected."

In the process of making *sparkling wines* the juice is separated from the husks as soon as the grapes are mashed. This is put into vats and racked off from time to time until the wine is clear; then it is carefully bottled, to within an inch or two of the top, and corked. The bottles are then placed in a horizontal position. When the sediment has settled upon the cork, the bottles are opened and the sediment let out, after which the bottles are filled, *corked* and *wired*. The sparkling qualities of the wine is increased by the addition of fine sugar, which, being dissolved in wine, is added to the wine when the bottles are opened.

Wines in casks must be drawn from the "*lees*" and put into clean vessels in order to prevent further fermentation and to improve the quality. In all cases the casks are to be filled and bunged tight.

Under the management of the enterprising corporators of the "Pleasant Valley Wine Company" the culture of grapes has been widely extended, and several individuals are erecting "*grape houses*" for the preservation of their crops through the winter for spring marketing in the different cities and villages. Strangers are coming into the valley to settle and to purchase land for vineyards.

It has been observed, by those who have examined different districts of the United States with a view to grape culture, that the shore of the Crooked lake presents superior advantages in respect to the vigor and health of the vine and in the freedom of its fruit from mould, mildew, or rot.

The waters of the lake being of great depth and fed by perennial springs of cold pure water, it is always, during the summer and autumn, much colder than the surrounding atmosphere, and, consequently, free from fogs, to which other localities are subject. The Hudson river, warmed by the tides flowing in from the ocean, is very much subject to a foggy atmosphere. The valleys through which small rivers and streams run are also subject, for the cause that the water becomes warm through the day, and the cold air of the nights or early morning becomes a medium of its evaporation in dense fogs that are very injurious to the growth and maturity of the grape.

The vineyards at and near Cincinnati, in Illinois, in Missouri, and indeed throughout all those localities where the causes above referred to are present, are subject to disease of the vine and of the fruit. In all these places we hear of the "*blight*" and of the "*mould*" and "*mildew.*" The peculiar state of the atmosphere, induced by fog, produces upon the vine and the grape the minute vegetable "*fibre*" or "*fungus*" which is known to naturalists under the denomination of "*mycelium,*" the "*spores*" of which contain the "*sporules,*" or seeds, which develop in time "*mould*" or "*oidium.*"

In the localities above referred to the parasitic fungus with which the vine is affected makes its appearance as a small blotch upon the surface of the leaf, and spreads so rapidly that in a few days every part of the vine is covered with minute "*spores.*" Each of these spores is a seed vessel containing thousands of seeds or "*sporules,*" all endowed with vegetable vitality, and the fruit of the vine is enveloped over its entire surface with a coating of mould, and the grape shrivels up, as if dried by the scorching sun. It becomes totally unfit for use either upon the table as a desert or for the manufacture of wine.

Pleasant Valley, and the Shore of the Crooked Lake, like KELLEY'S ISLAND, in Lake Erie, although in theory too far out of the "*Grape Zone,*" for the cultivation of that fruit, yet, in practice, the success has been all that could be desired. From the commencement of Grape Culture in 1855, nothing like a failure of the crop has occurred, and nothing like disease of the vine or of the fruit has been known to exist.

They who have cultivated vineyards, study the habit of the vine, as it appeared in this locality, and arrange their mode of culture accordingly. A little more space is allowed the vine to breathe in the pure air, and to receive the sunshine, and the grape sets, grows, and matures to great perfection.

Although the vine is a "*gross feeder,*" and will grow vigorously in rich soil, taking up its aliment in huge proportions, yet where the soil is in proper condition when "*set to grapes,*" it will produce several crops without much restoration by manure. A due caution is to be observed in this respect ; by overcharging the soil with fertilizers, a profuse growth of vine is induced, with small inferior crops, but the soil requires renovation from

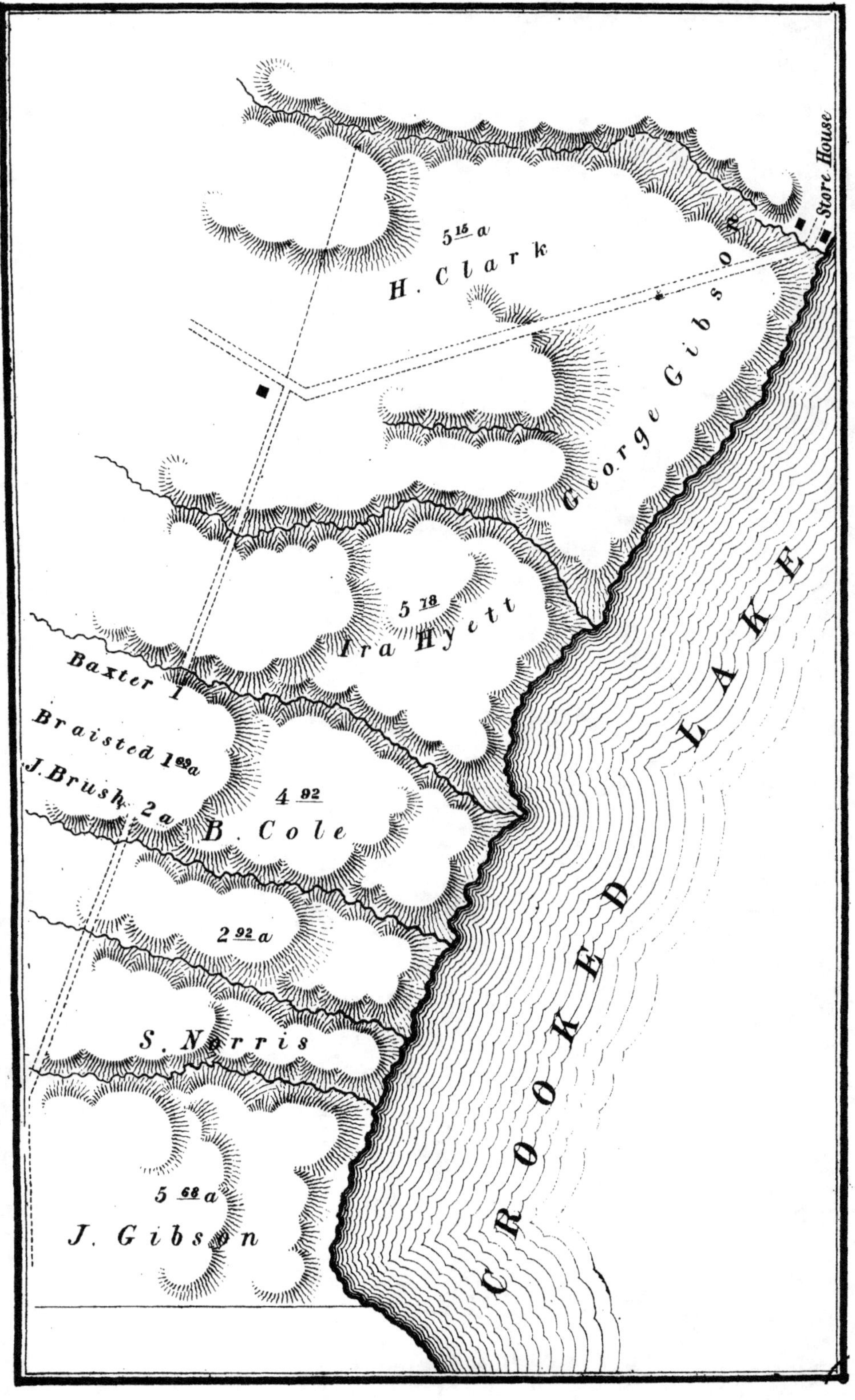

Store House
5 15 a
H. Clark
George Gibson
5 78
Ira Hyett
Baxter 1
Braisted 1
J. Brush 2 a
4 92
B. Cole
2 92 a
S. Norris
5 68 a
J. Gibson
CROOKED LAKE

time to time to prevent exhaustion, and experienced cultivators have found *marl* and *wood ashes* a good application after the fruit is gathered in autumn, and cattle manure mixed with litter, barley and oat straw. Straw of beans may be applied to advantage, as they all contain a considerable amount of *alkali.*

The vine is principally composed of lime, magnesia, alkali and phosphoric acid, and any ingredient containing lime and alkali furnishes proper manure. Bone black is a powerful manure for the vine as it is largely composed of phosphorous.

To loosen the soil straw plowed under, weeds and grass, especially clover, produces a fine tilth, and a free, open and loose soil.

Experience has demonstrated that compost, if not mixed with substances obnoxious to the vine, is the most suitable fertilizer, because it is deprived, by fermentation, of all *volatile ammoniacal* substances injurious to the vine. And all the other substances being dissolved are easily taken up and absorbed by the vine.

In order to make the compost, a pit, in some shady place, ought to be prepared, in which to put the fertilizing substances, such as animal and vegetable offal, ashes, straw, turf, sods, &c., &c., and the whole covered with earth; at times the whole should be turned, and sprinkled with water to produce a proper fermentation, and a solution of all the parts to perfect the mass for the application to the soil of the vineyard.

Too much care cannot be taken in the application of manure to the vine. Though gross in its appetite to take in food, yet it is extremely sensitive in the effects produced thereby. If ingredients enter therein obnoxious to the vine, it will readily develop the effects in its growth and production. Nitrogen in none of its conditions enter into the composition of the vine; not even its leaves, and shoots contain it, and manure containing nitrogen is injurious.

Upon the subject of manures for vineyards this general fact stands prominent—when the soil has become exhausted, the vines and the fruit become meagre, and the wine made therefrom thin and meagre, wanting body, and the peculiar flavor termed "*bouquet.*" Over-manured vineyards will make a great show of wood, tendrils and leaves, but the fruit will be *gumous*, and the wine made will become too *fat* and *smeary*. In this department of grape growing a discerning mind will discover the *medium* in which there is both safety and profit.

Grape Lands and Vineyards.

The stimulus given to grape culture by the success of the persons engaged therein, induced many others to purchase sites and to plant vineyards, not only in Pleasant Valley, but also along the west shore of the Crooked Lake. The extreme southern part of Pleasant Valley breaks through the hills westward, which in their southern slopes afford fine exposure for vineyards, and these hills are now being wholly occupied by the vine. The frequent *breaks* in the hills, caused by "*runs of water*" passing from their summits to the valley below, give that peculiar *contour* of *sur-*

face well adapted for grape culture, and a drainage of the soil necessary for such purpose.

There is a striking similarity of soil and of feature in these bluffs and hill sides occupied by vineyards, and, at the same time, a very great variety of outline, imparting much of the *picturesque* to the *rural* and the *useful.*

Pleasant Valley being rich in agricultural products, and the hills terraced in vineyards, presents a beautiful feature—a landscape in which rural beauties combine to please the eye, and an adaptation for products scarcely to be met with in so narrow a compass.

From Hammondsport, south west, for about two miles, the hills are covered with vineyards almost to their summits, and the area for grape culture will exceed *four hundred acres.* This is being rapidly appropriated, and the time is not far distant when the whole will present a "*terraced*" feature similar to the bluffs in the rear of Cincinnati.

As an illustration, we here present a map of the valley, and the adjacent hills which rise from four to eight hundred feet above the waters of the Crooked Lake.

Within the area of the above map the lands suitable for grape culture will exceed eight hundred acres, of which about *four hundred and fifty* (450) acres are in bearing, and the remainder set with vines.

The principal vineyard proprietors are A. Y. Baker, C. D. Champlin, J. H. Weber, T. M. Younglove, G. H. Wheeler, J. Larrowe, Geo. Shephard, Aaron Rosenkrans, John Allis, Mrs. Orlando Shepard, E. P. Smith, Benjamin Myrtle, Dugald Cameron, jr., James Covert, Bell & McMaster, S. B. Fairchild, A. D. Fairchild, Ed. Fairchild, Walter M. Moore, Delos Rose, Fred. Haase, J. Eckli, John M. Wheaton, A. Brundage, L. D. Hastings, Rev. J. Vorhis, A. J. Switzer, and D. Sandford. Within the range of the above vineyards the average yield per acre is about *three tons,* and the aggregate crop for the year 1864, will fall a little below that figure.

These vineyardists deem the Catawba, Isabella, Delaware, Diana, Concord and Hartford Prolific, the most profitable fruit for their soil and climate.

Northward from the section above described to the north line of the town of Urbana, are a fine range of grape lands, of the best exposure for vineyards. Of these Mr. Nobles has sixteen acres, and several small proprietors twenty-five acres, from off of the old COGSWELL farm, David Bailey owning the balance, and cultivating a fine vineyard of several acres.

Mr. J. Van Est has 72 acres, and D. Bailey on his home farm some forty acres suitable for grapes. Northward of which is the old SAMUEL DREW farm, of equal capacity for grape culture, some twelve acres being set.

The farm of the Peter Depue heirs presents an area of more than sixty acres adapted to vineyards of more than a half mile lake shore, and the Pine Point farm of 168 acres, every foot of which is intended to be set, and about eighty acres of the lands of David Hatchers, Esq.

In the south part of the town of Pulteney, vineyards are being set all along the shore of the Bedell farm to the extent of about *fifty acres.* Also of the Hyatt farm about thirty acres. North of which Joseph Hall has a fine vineyard, and can appropriate about twenty-five acres to the culture of grapes, and about the same area from the farm of the widow Brink. Next north is the farm of Amos Eggleston of more than seventy acres, the whole of which has been purchased for vineyard purposes, and some of it set with vines.

The middle district of the town of Pulteney extending from Bluff Port to Harmony Ville, includes some of the best grape lands along the lake shore. These are peculiarly adapted *by ravines* for division into separate vineyards, as is seen by the following map of the lands sold by Geo. Gibson to several proprietors.

Mr. Gibson has about sixty acres of grape land of a very choice quality, Captain Smith, twenty-five, and the Ed. Davis farm has all been bought for that purpose, as also the T. W. Boyd, and the French farms each containing about one hundred acres.

The Messrs. Cross has one of the best producing vineyards in the town. He has made the products very valuable on account of their perfect maturity and fine flavor. His Catawbas are particularly held in high estimation.

Larrowe & Hadden have bought the John Decker place all for grape culture sixty acres, and George S. Ellas, forty acres; north of whom lie the vineyards of Mr. Suttan, five acres; A. H. Denniston, thirty acres; Atwood, 10 acres; J. Neff, 7 acres; Roff, ten acres, and David Osborn an area of more than forty acres suitable for that purpose. All these vineyards are in fine bearing condition, and extremely profitable to their proprietors, yielding about four hundred dollars per acre annually.

From Harmony Ville, northward to the town line about four miles, lies a range of lake shore hills, with slope and exposure unsurpassed for vineyard purposes. Of the vineyards and lands of Mr. Prentice, Wixom and D. S. Wagener, we have given a description and a diagram. North of these are the vineyards of G. Morehouse and others, of ten acres; of Mrs. Alexander and C. Parker, of several acres.

The next farm, Peter Coon, of seventy-five acres, has been bought at $135 per acre, for grape culture.

About one month previous to the sale of this farm, we met Mr. Coon. He had been bantered to sell, but not aware of the excitement for grape lands estimated the land for agricultural purposes only, and put a moderate valuation upon it, but as he was so frequently approached by persons desirous to purchase, he began to think there was something of particular value in his land, and rose in price accordingly. Two years ago he would have sold for $50; one year ago for $80; three months ago for $100, and one month before selling for $125. He finally sold for $135. He said "he did not want to sell, but speculators would not let him keep it, no matter how much he asked, they would come up to his price, and he was tired of bidding up and they accepting, so to get rid of them he sold his farm." He has gone west where he thinks "grape speculators will not trouble him."

It is a fine farm with a peculiar warm exposure, and the present owners will make money out of it.

Mr. Robie has lately bought forty acres lying north of the Coon farm, of the same quality of land, and very suitable for grape culture, and Jacob Coryell has fifty acres of the same sort, but it will take shrewd management to induce him to sell at any price.

North of Mr. Coryell lies one hundred acres of a continuous slope to the lake shore, with ravines, knolls, and undulations particurlarly beautiful. It has one of the most desirable building sites throughout the whole range of the lake shore, and the soil is of the very best quality for grape culture. To the man of taste who would combine the "*useful with the beautiful*," we know of no place more appropriate.

This has lately been purchased by Edwin C. Barton, Esq., for vineyard purposes, and measures are being taken to set vines, in the spring. In passing over the land we were surprised at its singularly beautiful appearance and rich soil. To convey some idea of which we give the following map, drawn from actual survey.

When Mr. Barton has completed his vineyards and other improvements — these terraced hills and slopes — these knolls and gullies decked with the foliage of the vine — the evergreen and the oak will present a scene lovely and pleasant, indeed a landscape full of rural attractions and picturesque views.

North of these grounds lies the vineyard of Mrs. Phebe V. Bedell, and grounds of about fourteen acres; Arnold Stewart, twenty-five acres; J. Watrous, forty acres, and Mr. Miller and Chitsey, from eighty to one hundred acres of grape lands. They have commenced planting and a few years will extend the culture over all the area suitable for that purpose.

In this connection may be added some reference to the grape lands upon Bluff Point, in the county of Yates, upon the extreme southern part of the Point, Gregg, Vorhis & Nichols have ninety-two acres of a very fine exposure upon which a vineyard has been started. North of this are eighty acres owned by Pratt, Gillett and Wilkinson, and north of this two hundred acres owned by G. D. Michell, of which about eighty acres are fine for grapes. A. Brown owns twenty-seven acres, and still north two hundred and forty-five acres belonging to Thomas Van Tuyl of Plattsburgh, extending two miles along the lake shore and all adapted to grape growing. A large vineyard is to be set thereon the ensuing spring. One hundred acres north of this is being set, and for seven miles along the lake shore are a succession of farms containing in the aggregate about nine hundred acres suitable for the cultivation of the grape.

The above lands need no description as they are similar in soil and exposure to those already described in the vicinity of Harmony Ville.

North of the line of the town of Pulteney, upon the west branch of the lake, the grape lands extend to Branchport, in the town of Jerusalem, Yates co., and several vineyards have been started with flattering prospects of success.

The grape growing enterprise, though comparatively new, is destined to become a source of employment and of prosperity to a large number of our citizens. Aside from the ameliorating tendency it imparts to the taste in the department of agriculture, it will stimulate many to action who have heretofore "*plodded along in the old way*," unimproving and unimproved.

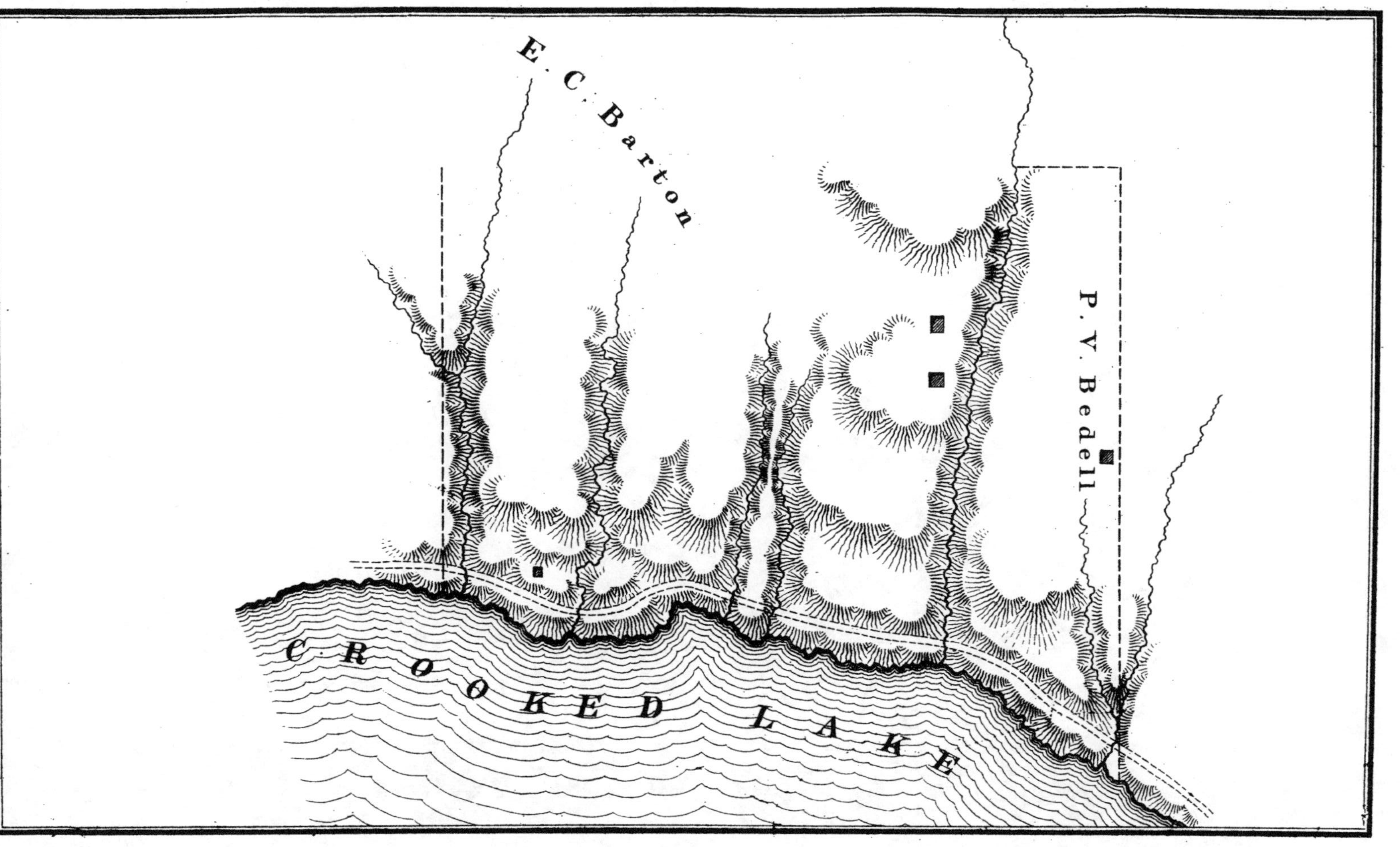

E. C. Barton
P. V. Bedell
CROOKED LAKE

A few years will find these lands beautifully laid out into vineyards, and adorned not only with the vine, but also with homes, around which will cluster all that can attract and beautify, and some, though humble, will become the center of all that can please the eye and gratify the taste.

Varieties of Grapes Cultivated.

During the incipient stages of grape culture, the Isabella was deemed the standard variety, as a hardy and productive vine, and as ripening somewhat earlier and more surely. The Isabella grape was named after Mrs. Isabella Gibbs, who first introduced the vine at the North. Mrs. Gibbs was the wife of Col. Geo. Gibbs, a merchant in New York city, and who resided at Brooklyn. The vine that was brought north and planted in his garden at Brooklyn, came from the Woodford plantation on Cape Fear River, in Brunswick county, N. C., belonging to his father, Mr. R. Gibbs. This vine grew rapidly, and bore fine crops of luscious fruit. It was when General Swift lived in the same house at Brooklyn that Wm. Prince saw it, gave it the name Isabella, and introduced cuttings and roots from it to public notice.

The Isabella is reputed in our vicinity as a hardy, thrifty and productive variety. It has a sweet, medicinal flavor—hardly as "*vinous* and *sprightly*" as some other varieties, and somewhat subject to rot. When not carefully preserved, has a musty taste, and is by no means equal to the Catawba either for table use or for wine.

There is a peculiar character of the Isabella, which is similar to some foreign varieties, and have induced the belief that it is of that origin. A Mr. J. Togno, a vine dresser of Wilmington, N. C., notices this in a communication on the subject. He states "that Mr. Laspeyre sold the grape in the market of Wilmington, *as a foreign grape*, and that it had all the character of a European variety ; that it would rot, and did rot with the first cultivators of it." The same complaint has been made of it by other cultivators at Cincinnati and elsewhere, but in the valley of the Crooked Lake it is still held in high favor as a productive and a marketable variety.

But the Catawba is deemed quite its superior in flavor and for the manufacture of wine. This grape has its origin in North Carolina. It is found growing wild on the Catawba River, in Lincoln county of that State. It was first introduced by Mr. Adlum, into cultivation at Georgetown, D. C., and from thence by Mr. Longworth to Cincinnati, Ohio. It was first named the "*Lincoln grape*," from the county where it was first found growing wild, but afterwards "*Catawba*," from the river, on the banks of which it was found growing.

The vines of the Catawba are hardy, strong and vigorous ; the leaves are large, and the wood of a reddish color. It is deemed the best wine, and table grape in the county. It does not ripen quite as early as the Isabella, but is of a more sprightly flavor, and will command a higher price in the market.

The Isabella and Catawba grapes are the standard varieties cultivated in the grape growing district of Steuben, and are found to be equally reliable with any other kind. They generally ripen in season to prevent being injured by frost; produce full crops; and are free from mildew, or any other disease that would impair their value.

They are also the standard varieties for the city markets; they sell readily, and command remunerative prices. At this present time the Catawba sells readily for *thirty cents* per pound, and extra fine bunches will bring *thirty-five cents.*

In all the market stalls for fruits these two varieties of grapes are found almost to the exclusion of others, and at the WINE PRESS they are preferred as producing the best of wine.

The Catawba grape is particularly adapted to the manufacture of good wine. It has a peculiar sprightly flavor that imparts to the wine an extra value in the estimation of connoiseurs. It is said that some of the low priced wines of Europe are bought up by our manufacturers and put upon the Catawba pommace after the juices are drawn of and allowed to ferment thereon to impart to them the peculiar tastes of that grape. These wines thus improved are sold at advanced prices "*as Catawba wine.*"

The *Diana* is of the same family of grapes as the Isabella and Catawba, as being "*vinous*" and "*sprightly.*" It is a seedling of the Catawba, of great purity of flavor, extremely *sweet* and *vinous*, and more free from astringency than the parent grape. This grape was originated by Mrs. Diana Crehor of Milton Hill, near Boston. It is extensively cultivated by vineyardists and is highly estimated for its productive habits, and peculiar fine flavor. It grows and produces finely in Pleasant Valley and along the shore of the Crooked Lake.

Another grape, a seedling of the Isabella, and of its peculiar color and bloom, is the "*Union Village,*" produced by the Shakers of that place. It will ripen about ten days earlier than the parent grape. It is of the size of the Black Hamburg, and is often mistaken for it. This grape is not extensively cultivated in our county, but is worthy of a place in every vineyard *as a wine grape.*

The *Delaware,* which had its origin at Delaware in Ohio, has often been awarded the premium "as the best native grape." It is of a smaller berry than the Catawba—is free from astringency—flesh very juicy with some consistence, and vinous and sprightly. It is *sweet—sweet to its very centre.*

The Delaware is very hardy. It will stand where other grapes have been killed to the ground. It is a great bearer, and will increase in productiveness as the vine is cultivated and grows older. It ripens early, more so than any other. The stock is somewhat difficult to propagate, consequently commands a high price.

It is highly esteemed as a small table grape and its wine is similar to the "*wines of the Rhine.*"

The Delaware, though not extenslvely cultivated in Steuben, is held in high estimation, and will, in time, receive more general attention as a standard variety of the very best.

The *Northern Muscadine* is of a "foxy," or rank-flavored variety. It ripens its fruit uneven, and the berries will drop as they ripen. It is not deemed a good variety for general cultivation.

The *Rebecca* is a seedling of the Isabella, grown by Mrs. Peake of Hudson.

It grows bunches of a medium size, very compact, color green in the shade, but of a lively amber in the sun, with a fine bloom. It is extremely sweet and luscious. It is a hardy variety, and ripens its fruit early and is well suited for extreme northern grape regions.

The *Hartford Prolific* is an early grape and extremely hardy. It is not equal to the Isabella in flavor, and is generally held in estimation only as a hardy variety, that will grow and produce when others will fail.

The *Concord* had it origin at Concord, Mass. It has proved perfectly hardy and healthy wherever cultivated. It grows bunches compact, berries large, almost black, and covered with bloom. The skin is thick, flesh juicy and sweet. It is a grape possessed of much "*aroma*," and is deemed good for wine. As this grape will grow in more exposed situations than many others it is worthy of attention.*

The *Clinton* is a hardy variety, grows moderately, is healthy, grows bunches small, with round compact berries of a black color and blue bloom. It is quite a rambling grower, with berries *too small* for vineyard purposes and a flavor too harsh for table use. It is cultivated to quite a limited extent in Pleasant Valley.

The *Iona* grape to which was awarded the Greely prize of $100, the requirements for which "being nothing less than a grape equal to the best European kinds, with a vine equal in hardiness of our most enduring native varieties," is well qualified to meet the requirements of the premium offered. This grape is a seedling produced by Dr. C. W. Grant of Iona Island, and is pronounced by the best lovers of good grapes as superior to any. This grape has been grown successfully in several parts of the State, and has received favorabe reports from all. It is held in high esteem wherever cultivated in our county.

For a *very early grape* the best is probably the *Isrealla,* a seedling also raised by Dr. Grant. The bunches of this grape are large, and the flesh tender and juicy and sweet. It is a good grower, hardy and productive. It is probably the best early table grape—fully equal in all respects to the Delaware.

The Urbana Wine Company, incorporated under the general law of the State, with a capital of $250,000, has been organized for the purpose of

---

* By a series of observations made for a number of years at Waterloo, N. Y., it has been seen that those varieties of grapes which had a mean temperature of 69° during the month following the *stoning process* were of a superior quality. Those that had 67° were inferior, and those which stoned so late as to have only 65° did not ripen. Of the first class were the Delaware, Clinton, Diana, Isabella and Rebecca. Of the second class were the Hartford Prolific, Union Village, Concord, Catawaba and the To Kalon, and of the class that did not ripen were the Anna, Y. Madeira, and Crevelling. From these observation the following deductions are made. That the Delaware and Clinton vines require a summer temperature of 66° 5', a hot month of 70°, and a September of 60°, or a mean for their growing season of 65°. The Concord, Hartford prolific and Diana require a mean of 67°, or a summer heat of 70°, a month of 72, and a September at 63°. The Isabella requires a mean of 72°, summer, 72°, one month, 73°, and a September, 65°. And the Catawba to ripen fully requires a mean during the growing season of 72°, or a summer mean of 73°, a hot month of 75, and a September of 65°. The European grapes require a summer mean of 74°, a hot month of 75°, and a September not lower than 75°, to ripen fully. A writer states: "The exceptions to the above are found at places *influenced by water*, whose high or moderate September mean may extend into October without intervening frosts."

manufacturing wines and brandies from the grape, for the production and culture of the best varieties. This company owns about fifty acres in vineyard, and the "Pine Point farm" of 168 acres, all of which is intended to be set. A steamboat landing is to be established on the Point, and vaults and buildings are to be erected thereon for the use of the association.

Another wine company is being organized in the town of Pulteney, for like purposes, the vaults and buildings of which are to be erected at or near George Gibson's, where a wharf, store house and a steamboat landing is now established.

G. DENNISTON.

INDEX.

www.ingramcontent.com/pod-product-compliance
Lightning Source LLC
LaVergne TN
LVHW011122110826
845150LV00008B/2224

* 9 7 8 1 4 1 8 1 9 5 5 6 4 *